Lives and Times

Florence Nightingale

Emma Lynch

Heinemann Library
Chicago, Illinois

Designed by Richard Parker and Tinstar Design Ltd (www.tinstar.co.uk)
Originated by Repro Multi Warna
Printed and bound in China by South China Printing Company

09 08 07 06 05
10 9 8 7 6 5 4 3 2 1

Library of Congress Cataloging-in-Publication Data
Lynch, Emma.
   Florence Nightingale / Emma Lynch.
      p. cm. -- (Lives and times)
   Includes bibliographical references and index.
   ISBN 1-4034-6352-2 (library binding-hardcover) -- ISBN 1-4034-6366-2 (pbk.) 1. Nightingale, Florence, 1820-1910--Juvenile literature. 2. Nurses--England--Biography--Juvenile literature. I. Title. II. Series: Lives and times (Des Plaines, Ill.)
   RT37.N5L96 2005
   610.73'092--dc22
                              2004017437

Acknowledgments
The author and Publisher are grateful to the following for permission to reproduce copyright material: pp. 4, 6, 7, 19, 20, 21, 23, 24, 26, 27 The Florence Nightingale Museum Trust; pp. 5, 12, 16 Mary Evans Picture Library; pp. 8, 10 Hulton Archive/Getty Images; p. 9 National Portrait Gallery; pp. 11, 13, 15, 18 The Wellcome Trust Medical Photograhic Library; p. 14 London Stills; p. 17 P&O Art Collection; p. 22 The National Army Museum; p. 25 Guy Stubbs/Corbis/ Gallo Images. Page icons Hemera Objects

Cover photograph of Florence Nightingale, reproduced with permission of The Wellcome Trust Medical Photographic Library.

Photo research by Melissa Allison and Fiona Orbell

Special thanks to Rebecca Vickers for her comments in the preparation of this book.

Every effort has been made to contact copyright holders of any material reproduced in this book. Any omissions will be rectified in subsequent printings if notice is given to the Publisher.

Contents

Some words are shown in bold, **like this**. You can find out what they mean by looking in the glossary.

Who Was Florence Nightingale?

Florence Nightingale was a famous nurse. She lived in the 1800s. People did not think nursing was an important job then. Florence made it very important.

This is Florence when she was 36 years old.

Florence took care of soldiers who were hurt in a war. She started the first nursing school in Great Britain. She also wrote a book for nurses about how to care for people.

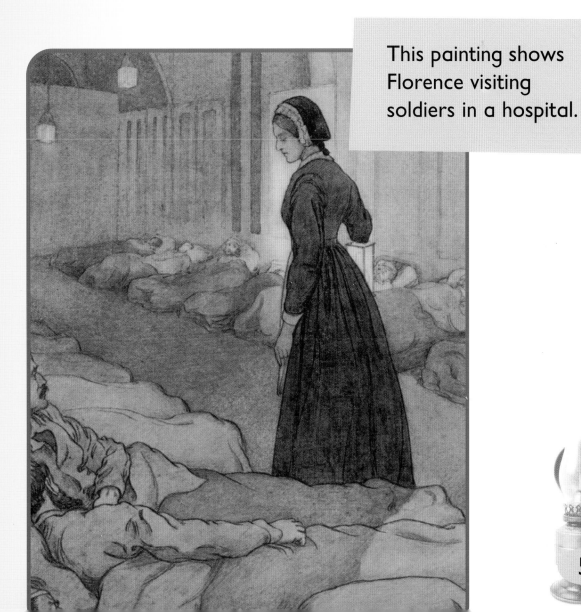

This painting shows Florence visiting soldiers in a hospital.

A Happy Childhood

Florence Nightingale was born on May 12, 1820. Her parents were visiting Italy. She was named Florence because she was born in a city in Italy named Florence.

This is Florence's father, William Nightingale. Florence's older sister, Parthenope, is sitting down.

In 1825 Florence's family moved to this house in Hampshire, England.

The family came back to England in 1821. Florence and her sister Parthenope were taught their school lessons at home. Florence was very good at math.

Planning Her Future

Florence grew into a young woman. Her parents wanted her to get married. They did not want her to have a job. Rich women did not work then.

This is a painting of Florence and Parthenope when they were young women.

On February 7, 1837, Florence believed she heard God's voice asking her to work for him. She decided not to get married. She wanted to work for God.

When Richard Monckton Milnes asked Florence to marry him, she said no.

Caring for Others

In the 1800s, many people died from diseases like **cholera**. Florence wanted to help sick people. She became sure that God wanted her to be a nurse.

When Florence was young, sick people were not cared for very well.

Florence heard about a special hospital in Germany. It trained nurses. Nurses in England were not trained at that time. Nursing was not a **respectable** job.

This old cartoon makes fun of nurses.

Florence Becomes a Nurse

Florence's parents did not want her to be a nurse. They tried to stop her many times. This upset her so much that she became ill. Her parents sent her on a vacation.

Florence visited beautiful places, like this, when she was on vacation.

In 1850 Florence went to visit the special hospital in Germany. When her parents found out, they punished her—even though she was 30 years old!

In 1851 Florence was allowed to train at the **Institution** of **Deaconesses** at Kaiserwerth in Germany.

Starting Work

When Florence came home, a friend found her a job. She would run a small hospital. Florence's father was still angry, but he agreed to give her some money to live on.

The hospital was on Harley Street in London.

FLORENCE NIGHTINGALE LEFT HER HOSPITAL ON THIS SITE FOR THE CRIMEA · OCTOBER 21ST 1854

Florence started work on August 12, 1853. She had many new ideas for the hospital. Her biggest problem was that there were no trained nurses to help her.

Hospitals looked like this when Florence was a nurse.

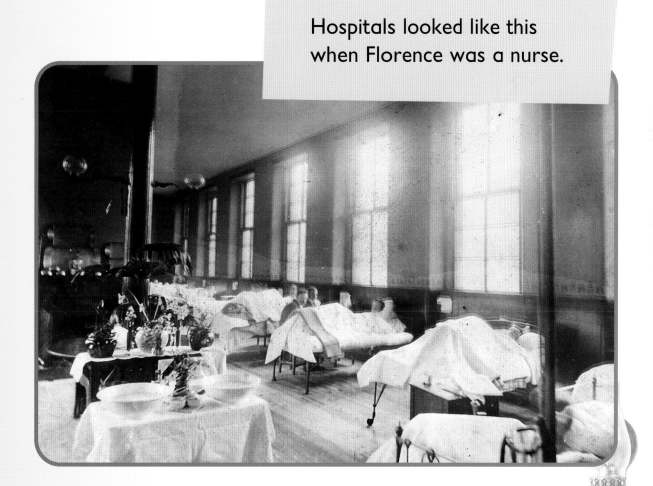

The Crimean War

In 1854 British soldiers went to fight in the **Crimean War**. Soldiers that were hurt were taken to army hospitals at Scutari, in Turkey.

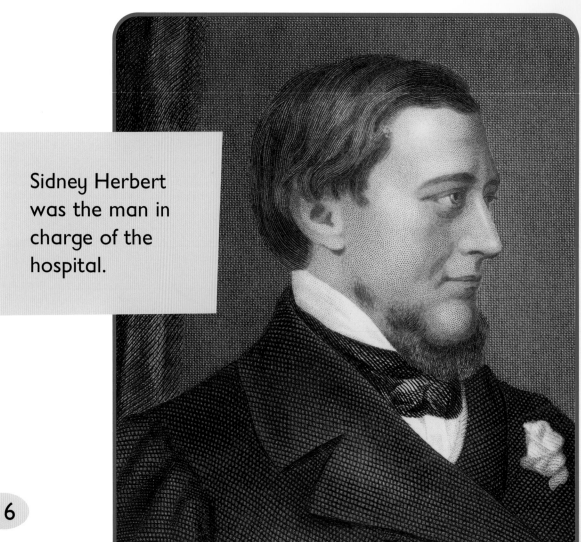

Sidney Herbert was the man in charge of the hospital.

Florence and her nurses sailed to Turkey on this ship. It was called *The Vectis*.

Sidney Herbert asked Florence to find nurses to go and help the soldiers. Florence left London on October 21, 1854. She went to Scutari with 38 other nurses.

17

The Hospital at Scutari

Florence arrived at the hospital on November 5, 1854. It was a terrible place. Rats were everywhere. The toilets were just dirty holes in the ground.

The hospital at Scutari was called the Barrack Hospital.

There was no **furniture**, and nothing to cook with. Florence made sure that the hospital was clean. She **organized** workers and ordered **supplies**.

At night, Florence walked through the hospital with a lamp to check that her **patients** were comfortable.

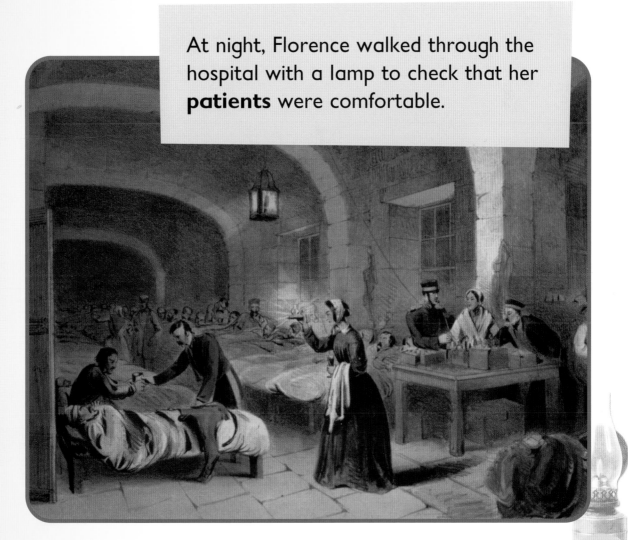

Florence Is a Heroine!

Florence came back to Britain in 1856. She was a **heroine**. She met Queen Victoria in October 1856. Florence wrote an important report about what she had seen in the war.

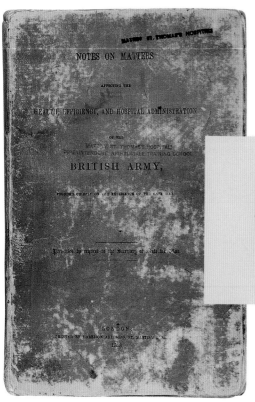

People read Florence's report. After that they made **hygiene** better in the army and in hospitals.

On June 24, 1860, Florence opened the Nightingale Training School for nurses. It was at St. Thomas' Hospital in London. She had made nursing a **respectable** job.

Florence gave these gifts to the nurses at her school.

The End of a Good Life

Florence took care of other people all her life. She became ill herself and went blind in 1901. Florence was given many **awards** for her work.

Florence was the first woman to be given the **Order of Merit**. She received it in 1907.

This is Florence when she was older.

Florence died on August 13, 1910, when she was 90 years old. A service was held at St. Paul's Cathedral in London. People wanted to remember her life.

Why Is Florence Famous?

Florence believed that nurses should be trained to care for their **patients**. They should make sure that patients are always kept clean and comfortable.

Florence is sitting with the nurses at the Nightingale Training School.

Florence also helped improve **hygiene**. She knew that hospitals should be kept clean to stop **germs** from spreading. She made life better for people in army hospitals.

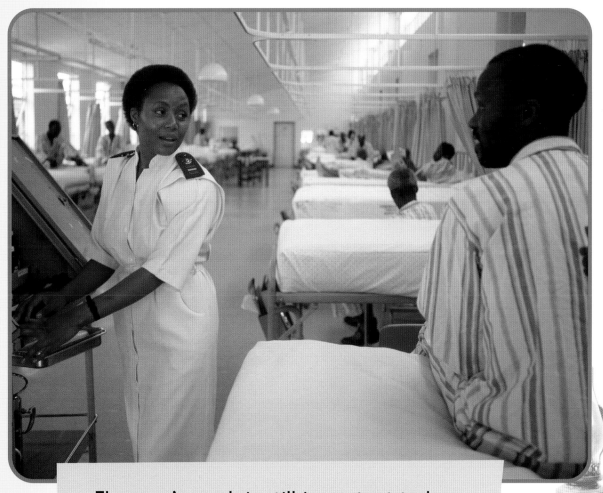

Florence's work is still important today.

More About Florence

There are many ways to find out about Florence. There are books, websites, and **museums** about her life and work. We can also hear a recording of her voice.

We can still see Florence's lamp in a museum today.

We can find out more from Florence's own writing. She wrote letters, reports, and books, and kept a diary. She even wrote notes all through her childhood.

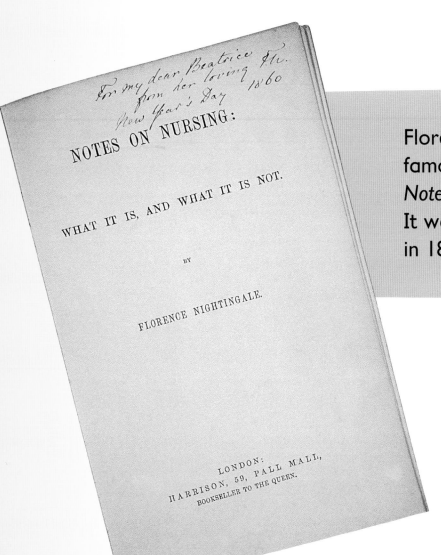

For my dear Beatrice &c. from her loving New Year's Day 1860

NOTES ON NURSING:

WHAT IT IS, AND WHAT IT IS NOT.

BY

FLORENCE NIGHTINGALE.

LONDON:
HARRISON, 59, PALL MALL,
BOOKSELLER TO THE QUEEN.

Florence's most famous book was *Notes on Nursing*. It was printed in 1859.

Fact File

- When Florence was a young woman, several men asked her to marry them. One of them was Richard Monckton Milnes. She would not marry him, but she always stayed friends with him.

- During the **Crimean War**, Florence walked around the hospital every night. She always carried a lamp. She wanted to make sure her **patients** were comfortable. Because of this, she was called "the lady with the lamp."

- Some nurses and churches celebrate Florence Nightingale's life on or around May 12 every year. They would like this to become Florence Nightingale Day.

Timeline

1820   Florence is born in Florence, Italy, on May 12

1837   Florence thinks she hears God talking to her

1842   Florence finds out about the special hospital at Kaiserwerth in Germany

1851   Florence trains for three months in Kaiserwerth

1854   Florence travels to Scutari in Turkey She takes care of soldiers hurt in the **Crimean War**

1856   Florence returns to Great Britain.

1860   The Nightingale Training School for nurses opens at St. Thomas' Hospital in London

1907   Florence is the first woman to receive the **Order of Merit**

1910   Florence dies on August 13

Glossary

award prize for doing something good

cholera disease that people catch from bad food or dirty water

Crimean War war fought by Great Britain and France against Russia between 1853 and 1856. Great Britain and France won the war.

deaconess woman who works for a church

furniture things for the home, such as beds, chairs, and tables

germ something that can make you ill

heroine woman who is brave or good

hygiene keeping people and things clean and healthy

institution place where people go to learn

museum building where pieces of art or items from history are kept

Order of Merit award given by the Queen of England

organize to plan to make something happen

patient someone who is cared for by a doctor or nurse

respectable good, well behaved, and honest

supplies things that people need, such as food or medicine

More Books to Read

Schaefer, Lola M. *Florence Nightingale.*
Bloomington, MN: Capstone Press Inc., 2004.

Vickers, Rebecca. *Florence Nightingale.*
Minneapolis, MN: Sagebrush Education
Resources, 2003.

Places to Visit
Florence Nightingale Museum
St. Thomas' Hospital
2 Lambeth Palace Road
London, UK

Index